Foods of Poland

Barbara Sheen

KIDHAVEN PRESS
A part of Gale, Cengage Learning

GALE
CENGAGE Learning™

Detroit • New York • San Francisco • New Haven, Conn • Waterville, Maine • London

GALE
CENGAGE Learning™

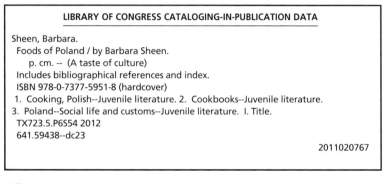

LIBRARY OF CONGRESS CATALOGING-IN-PUBLICATION DATA

Sheen, Barbara.
  Foods of Poland / by Barbara Sheen.
      p. cm. -- (A taste of culture)
  Includes bibliographical references and index.
  ISBN 978-0-7377-5951-8 (hardcover)
  1. Cooking, Polish--Juvenile literature. 2. Cookbooks--Juvenile literature.
  3. Poland--Social life and customs--Juvenile literature. I. Title.
  TX723.5.P6S54 2012
  641.59438--dc23

2011020767

Kidhaven Press
27500 Drake Rd.
Farmington Hills MI 48331

ISBN-13: 978-0-7377-5951-8
ISBN-10: 0-7377-5951-8

Printed in the United States of America
1 2 3 4 5 6 7 15 14 13 12 11

Printed by Bang Printing, Brainerd, MN, 1ˢᵗ Ptg., 09/2011

Contents

What the Land Has to Offer

Poland is a nation in central Europe with a harsh northern climate characterized by long snowy winters. It is blessed with rich soil in which crops that do not require a lengthy growing season flourish. In the past, the Polish people spent most of the year cultivating, gathering, storing, and preserving food to help them survive the winter. These foods included grains, hearty vegetables, mushrooms, and pork. Modern Polish people no longer live this way. They can purchase fresh food in supermarkets year-round. Even with many more foods to choose from, Poles still turn to these staple ingredients to create delicious meals.

Owing to the rich, fertile soil, Poland's abundant crops have a shorter harvest time.

"Without Bread There is No Dinner"

Plains cover most of the country. In fact, the name *Poland* means land of plains. Grains such as rye, wheat, and barley flourish there. Since grains can be stored in airtight containers for long periods without spoiling, they have always been a key source of food for the Polish people.

Polish cooks use grains to stuff cabbage leaves, thicken gravies, and top casseroles. They turn them into cereals, noodles, dumplings, pastries, and, most importantly, bread. According to an old Polish proverb, "Without bread there is no dinner."[1] No meal is considered complete without it. Bread is so important to the Polish people, if a piece is dropped on the ground, it is traditional to pick it up and kiss it.

Most Poles are Catholics and bread serves as a religious symbol for them. In the past, the sign of the cross was often carved into breads before they were baked. Bread is also a symbol of hospitality in Poland. It is customary to serve it to guests. "It's the most basic food," explained Michal, a Polish blogger. "Fresh bread symbolized a successful harvest and...the spirit of togetherness."[2]

Polish bakers make more than one hundred different types of bread. Dark and light rye breads, either plain or filled with sunflower seeds, are especially popular. But

Bread is very important to the Polish people. It is customary to have it with every meal, whether as a fresh baked loaf, or as day-old breadcrumbs mixed into fillings and topping vegetables.

no matter the variety, most Polish breads have a thick chewy crust and a soft moist interior.

Poles prefer freshly baked bread. But less-than-fresh bread is never wasted. It is turned into bread crumbs. They are fried with butter, parsley, and hard-boiled eggs and spread on top of cooked vegetables to create a delicious topping that is known to the world as vegetables Polonaise (Po-lon-aze).

Hearty Vegetables

Whether served Polonaise style or in another manner, vegetables such as cabbage, beets, cucumbers, carrots, cauliflower, and potatoes, which thrive in Poland's short growing season and can be preserved or stored for the winter, are vital to the Polish diet.

In the past, Poles preserved vegetables in many ways. They stored them in an underground room known as a root cellar; they laid them over a wood-burning stove to dry; or they pickled them. Pickled vegetables such as sauerkraut and dill pickles are favorites. Sauerkraut is made with cabbage, and pickles are made with cucum-

The Center of the Home

In the past, the stove served as the center of the Polish home. The family gathered around it for warmth and food. It stood in the corner of the main room. Stairs led from the stove to a loft on top of it. Here children or elderly family members slept. It was the warmest place in the house.

The stove was quite large, taking up most of the room. It had a large hood, which led to the chimney, an oven for baking, a stove top for cooking, ledges for holding matches, and little shelves, which served as a home for baby chicks, rabbits, or a hen during the winter.

The stove was fueled with wood or peat, decaying vegetation that formed in wet areas. Later, coal was used. Today, Poles have modern stoves fueled by gas or electricity.

Cauliflower Polonaise

Any fresh or frozen vegetable can be made Polonaise style. Just cook the vegetable and top it with the butter–bread crumb mixture. This recipe uses frozen cauliflower. Carrots, asparagus, broccoli, Brussels sprouts, cabbage, or spinach could be substituted.

Ingredients
16-ounce package of frozen cauliflower
3 tablespoons butter
3 tablespoons bread crumbs
1 egg, hard-boiled, chopped
1 tablespoon parsley, chopped

Instructions
1. Cook the cauliflower following the directions on the package.
2. Melt the butter over low heat. Stir in the bread crumbs. Cook until the bread crumbs are warm.
3. Add egg and parsley to bread crumb mixture and stir well.
4. Drain the cauliflower. Put it into a bowl. Pour the bread crumb mixture over it.

Serves 4.

A Polish vegetable dish topped with fried bread crumbs and egg is called vegetables Polonaise.

bers. The vegetables are placed in large barrels with salt, water, and various herbs and spices such as garlic, dill, and mustard grains. The salt **ferments** the vegetables and converts their natural juices into a sharp tangy liquid, which gives them their distinctive sour flavor.

Potatoes, too, are Polish favorites. Potatoes originated in Peru. Spanish explorers returning from the Americas introduced the vegetable to Europe in the 16th century. Potatoes grew very well in Poland's soil and climate. Even a tiny plot produced enough potatoes to keep a large family well fed. Potatoes soon became an essential part of the Polish diet. Modern Poles eat approximately 300 pounds (136kg) of potatoes per person per year.

Polish cooks use all of these vegetables in soups, salads, sauces, casseroles, and dumplings. They also serve them as appetizers and side dishes. Potato soup, cabbage with sour cream, and sweet-and-sour beets are just a few popular dishes.

A Wild Gift

Mushrooms, another favorite food, grow wild in Polish forests. Poles have been harvesting this wild gift for centuries. Mushroom hunting is an early autumn ritual in Poland. During that time, Poles flock to the forests to gather mushrooms. The adults teach the children which mushrooms are edible. At the same time, everyone enjoys the fresh air and the fall colors. "People in Poland love it," Mat, the author of Tasting Poland, a website all about Polish food, explained. "There are forests where in weekends you will find so many cars…that it looks like a parking lot."[3]

Once the mushrooms are gathered, they are sorted and cleaned. Some are freshly cooked, while others are preserved by pickling or drying. To dry mushrooms, a cook will gather about two dozen mushrooms and tie one to another with cord to form a wreath. The wreaths are hung on the sunny side of the house to dry. The cook plucks off dried mushrooms and soaks them in water to re-form them. Then, the mushrooms are used just like fresh mushrooms.

In Poland, people have been gathering wild mushrooms each fall for centuries.

Mushrooms in Sour Cream

This is a popular Polish side dish. Greek yogurt or low-fat yogurt can be substituted for full-fat sour cream.

Ingredients
1 pound of mushrooms
1 small onion, sliced
3 tablespoons butter
1 cup sour cream
1 tablespoon chopped dill
salt and pepper to taste

Instructions
1. Gently wash and dry the mushrooms. Cut off any tough ends. Slice the mushrooms.
2. Heat the butter in a pan over medium heat. When the butter is melted, add the mushrooms and onions. Fry until the onions are clear and the mushrooms are golden.
3. Stir in the sour cream, dill, salt, and pepper.
Serves 4

Mushrooms are the basis for gravies and soups. With their hearty taste and texture, they are popular substitutes for meat on days when meat is not allowed because of religious reasons. The earthy scent of mushrooms is a hallmark of Polish cooking. According to author Mary Pininska, "In Warsaw [the capital of Poland]… there is often a wonderful smell of cooked mushrooms pervading the cobbled streets."[4]

Popular Pork

The aroma of cooking meat, too, is a common scent in Polish kitchens. Most Poles like meat, with pork being a local favorite. Pigs are native to Poland. Long ago, wild pigs were hunted for meat. Over time, the animals were domesticated. In the past, almost every Polish family kept a pig, which was slaughtered in the fall. Some of the meat was catcn fresh, but most was preserved for the winter in the form of **kielbasa** (keel-bah-sa), or sausage. Historians think ancient Roman traders who traveled to Poland seeking **amber** and furs introduced sausage making to Polish cooks. By the Middle Ages, sausage making had become an art in Poland. To make sausage, Polish cooks stuffed casings made from pigs' intestines with a mixture of chopped pork, salt, pepper, garlic, and **marjoram**. The salt and spices preserved the meat. To give the sausages a woodsy taste and fragrance, some, but not all, were smoked by hanging them inside a chimney while a fire burned in the hearth.

Most modern Poles no longer make their own sausages. They buy them ready-made in butcher shops. There are dozens of varieties to choose from—long and small sausages, peppery sausages, sausages stuffed with pork and juniper berries, and sausages filled with pig's blood, to name a few.

The parts of the pig that are not used in sausages are also eaten. Poles enjoy pig's feet with mushrooms, pig's kidneys with buckwheat, and pork fat mixed with

Polish people no longer have to hunt or raise their own pigs for meat. Instead they can choose from a variety of sausages and smoked pork at their local butcher's shop.

fried onions and spices. Poles like to spread the spiced fat on bread. "When you go to a restaurant in Poland, it is almost the custom to be served fresh country bread on a wooden chopping board with...**smalec** [pig fat]," explained Michal. "And all that before you even managed to look at the menu."[5]

Whatever is on the menu, it is likely that it has been raised on Poland's rich soil. For centuries, Polish cooks have taken advantage of what their land had to offer. In so doing, they created many delicious dishes.

Chapter 2

Delicious and Hearty

An old Polish saying advises people to "Eat, drink, and loosen your belt."[6] Poles love hearty foods. The Polish people's favorite dishes certainly fit the bill. Dishes such as soups, noodles, dumplings, hunter's stew, and cabbage rolls are filling, tasty, and nutritious.

Soup Starts the Meal

Poles like to start a meal with a bowl of **zupa** (zoo-pah) or soup. And, when soup is served over boiled potatoes, accompanied by a hunk of fresh bread, it is a meal in itself. Poles eat soup for breakfast, lunch, and supper. "Each nation has its particular or proper food without which the daily meal would be incomplete,"

A Polish soup, or zupa, called kapusniak is made with sauerkraut, mushrooms, onions, and chunks of bacon, sausage (shown), or ham.

explained Polish author Rysia. "Italians would not go without spaghetti, the Chinese without rice, the Poles without a bowl of hot soup."[7]

Polish cooks make dozens of different types of soups. Most are loaded with vegetables, meat, and potatoes. **Kapusniak** (kah-poos-nee-ack), or cabbage soup, is a longtime favorite. It contains sauerkraut, mushrooms, onions, and chunks of bacon, sausage, or ham. The soup is thickened with flour, or more traditionally, flour fried with pork fat, which gives it a rich meaty taste. It is tart, thick, and warming, making it especially popular on cold winter days. Kapusniak is usually served over boiled potatoes. Some people like to add a squeeze of lemon to their soup to make it even more tart.

Krupnik (kroop-nick) is another top choice. It combines barley, dried mushrooms, potatoes, and beef or pork. Depending on the cook, other vegetables, such as celery, leeks, and carrots, may find their way into the pot, but barley is the main ingredient. It is one of the oldest grains grown in Poland. Poles have been eating it in krupnik for centuries. The soup is usually topped with a spoonful of thick fresh sour cream. The result is a heavy, satisfying soup with a fresh earthy aroma and a wholesome taste. It is like something a grandmother would make. According to Polish culture expert Barbara Swiech, "One bowl of krupnik soup will definitely make you full. It is a proper first dish or even the main dish on the table. It is surely better for cold winter evenings than in summer."[8]

Kapusniak

It is easy to be creative with this soup. It can be made on the stove top or in a slow cooker. Smoked beef, pork, or turkey sausage can be used. The base can be water, chicken, vegetable, or beef broth.

Ingredients
1 cup sauerkraut, drained
1 small onion, diced
2 medium potatoes, peeled and cut into chunks
1 cup carrots, peeled and cut into chunks
¾ pound smoked sausage, cut in chunks
6 cups low-sodium chicken broth
1 teaspoon black pepper

Instructions
1. Put all the ingredients in a slow cooker. Cook on high 4 hours or on low 8 hours.
Serves 4–6.

Lots of Appetizers

Poles often serve an array of hot and cold appetizers before a meal, especially on festive occasions. They also like to greet guests with tasty little treats. And sometimes Poles enjoy a large number of different appetizers as a meal. Popular appetizers include open-faced sandwiches. They are usually made on small squares of light or dark rye bread and are topped with whatever is on hand at the time. Chopped egg mixed with sweet pickles; cottage cheese, onion, and sliced radish; herring, hard-boiled egg and tomato; and ham, dill pickle, and mayonnaise, are just a few popular toppings. Other appetizers are heartier. They include dishes such as tiny meat pies; little dumplings and pancakes stuffed with meat or sauerkraut; cheese or sauerkraut patties; omelets with mushrooms or ham; pickled herring in sour cream sauce; macaroni, sausage, and peas; or chopped liver.

In the summer, Poles enjoy cold soups. Some feature freshly picked vegetables that are chilled in buttermilk, a sour liquid that is left after cream is churned into butter. Other cold soups are made with fruit and flavored with sugar, cinnamon, and sour cream. Apple soup, wild strawberry soup, and cherry soup are summer favorites.

Robust Stew

Poles like stew almost as much as they do soup. **Bigos** (bee-gus), or hunter's stew, is Poland's national dish. Poles have been eating this robust stew since ancient times. Originally, bigos was made in a big copper pot over an open fire by hunters who threw in chunks of freshly killed wild game along with sauerkraut and sausage. In the past, hunting was a popular pastime of Polish noblemen. They rode horses, dressed in bright red suits, and were led by a horseman tooting a horn to announce the start of the hunt. Modern Polish hunters are much more casual, but the tradition of making hunter's stew over a campfire has not changed.

Bigos is also made in Polish kitchens with meat purchased in butcher shops. The ingredients vary, making bigos a handy way to use leftovers.

Bigos, a stew made with sauerkraut, mushrooms, tomatoes, sugar, apples, and a variety of smoked or fresh meats, is the national dish of Poland.

Wild Game

Poland's forests are filled with wild game. For this reason, hunting has always been a popular pastime in Poland, and throughout history wild game has been a part of the Polish people's diet. Wild boar, which are large wild pigs, deer, and hare are commonly eaten. So are birds such as quail, partridge, pheasants, and wild ducks. In the past, Poles hunted on horseback. Modern Poles hunt on foot accompanied by hunting dogs that help them flush out the game. Game is so abundant in Poland that there are organized hunting expeditions for tourists.

Wild game is prepared much like farm-raised meat or poultry. Since the meat is often tougher than farm-raised animals, it is usually marinated in liquid flavored with spices and juniper berries, which tenderizes it, or makes it easier to chew. The meat is used in soups, stews, and casseroles. It is baked, roasted, and broiled.

Polish forests are abundant in wildlife. Hunting game, such as wild boar, is a popular activity.

Typically, the stew contains a variety of smoked and fresh meats, sauerkraut, mushrooms, tomatoes, sugar, and apples, which gives it an interesting mixture of sweet, sour, salty, and smoky flavors and an enticing aroma. The dish is so loved that a poem by Polish poet Adam Mickiewicz pays tribute to it. "No words," the poem says of the stew, "can tell the wonders of its color, taste and smell."[9]

Noodles and Dumplings

Noodles and dumplings are other popular favorites. Polish cooks make a variety of delicious noodle and dumpling dishes that are served both as main and side dishes. Egg noodles cooked with ham, mushrooms, or poppy seeds; hearty potato dumplings; and **uszka** (oosz-kah) or little ears, tiny dumplings filled with meat or mushrooms, are just a few. The most popular are **pierogi** (pyeh-raw-ghee).

Pierogi are half-moon–shaped dumplings stuffed with a wide variety of savory or sweet fillings. Savory fillings include potatoes, cheese, cabbage, sauerkraut, mushrooms, or ground meat, either alone or in numerous combinations. Fruit, soft cheese, or poppy seeds are popular sweet fillings. Size and shape vary, too. They are typically half-moon shaped, but they also can be round. Some pierogi are as large as dinner plates, while others are small and dainty. Every Polish cook has his or her own special recipe, which is passed from one generation to the next. Krissie, the author of a Polish cooking blog, explains the recipe she uses "was handed down to me by my grandmother and mother, with many hours of watching time under my belt—watching my gran that is, knead and roll out hundreds of pierogi in days gone by. She used to give me a board and a small rolling pin and some dough to practice on."[10]

Poles have been making pierogi for centuries. Some historians think the dumplings originated in Russia and were brought to Poland by a Russian princess who married into a wealthy Polish family. "Whatever their origins," Knab explained, "there is no dish more closely associated with Polish country cooking than pierogi."[11]

To make pierogi, cooks first make thin stretchy dough out of flour, butter, sour cream, and eggs. The filling is prepared and then spooned onto the dough. For meat filling, ground meats are fried with onions, bacon, pepper, and bread crumbs. For potatoes and cheese, hot mashed potatoes are mixed with fried onions and chunks of sharp cheese, which melts on the potatoes. Once filled, pierogies are folded closed and dropped into boiling water. When they float to the top, they are done. They may be served directly from the pot. Or, the

Pierogi are Polish dumplings with either savory fillings, like potato and cheese topped with bacon (shown), or sweet fillings, like fruit, soft cheese or poppy seeds.

Noodles and Ham

This is a popular Polish main dish. Cooked turkey or chicken can be substituted for ham.

Ingredients
½ pound cooked egg noodles
2 cups cooked ham, diced
2 tablespoons melted butter
1 egg, beaten
1 teaspoon dill (optional)
2 tablespoons bread crumbs

Instructions
1. Preheat the oven to 350 degrees.
2. Mix all the ingredients, except the bread crumbs, together.
3. Spray a baking dish with nonstick spray. Add the noodle mix. Sprinkle the bread crumbs on top.
4. Bake for 40–45 minutes until the casserole is hot and bubbly.

Serves 4.

cooked dumplings may be baked or fried in butter. They are usually topped with melted pork fat, butter, fried onions, or sour cream, all of which add rich flavor to the already yummy treats.

Stuffed Cabbage

Stuffed cabbage or **golabki** (ga-wump-kee) is another delicious and hearty dish that Poles have been eating for about 1,000 years. It is served in homes, restaurants, and on Polish military bases. In fact, in the 15th century when Polish soldiers defeated a large force of Ger-

Stuffed cabbage, called golabki, is a popular dish in Poland.

Foods of Poland

man invaders, they attributed their victory to the fact that they ate so much golabki. It, they said, gave them strength and energy.

To make golabki, cooks soften cabbage leaves by boiling them. Then they fill the leaves with ground pork, onions, and rice. They roll up the leaves to form plump cylinders and top them with sweet tangy tomato sauce. The whole thing is slowly baked until the cabbage leaves are silky and tender, the filling is steaming, and the sauce tastes of meat, tomatoes, and cabbage.

Golabki is typically served with bread, fried potatoes, and pickled beets. Richard A. Slowik, a member of Spuscizna, a group dedicated to spreading Polish culture, recalled the golabki he ate in Warsaw. It was, he said, "the best golabki I ever ate... It just melted in my mouth...I enjoyed each and every morsel."[12]

Poles enjoy many simple hearty dishes like golabki, pierogi, bigos, and soup. They are just the thing to satisfy a robust appetite and warm the body on cold windy days.

Fine Pastries

Polish pastries are world famous. Most Polish cities have a bakery on almost every street corner. Their windows are filled with an enticing array of beautiful layer cakes, richly aromatic coffee cakes, crisp and soft cookies, and dainty little open pies known as tarts. Home baking is also popular. Polish cooks pride themselves on their baking. In the past, according to author Alina Zeranska, "Talented housewives were famous all over the country and a lass who could produce an excellent **torte** [layer cake] would expect an excellent marriage."[13] Modern Polish homes are rarely without pastries. Poles eat them for dessert and as a snack with

Bakeries are abundant in Poland, providing world-famous Polish pastries for any occasion.

a steaming cup of tea or coffee. Pastries are also kept on hand to greet unexpected guests.

Cheesecake

Polish farmers are proud of their dairy products. Pastries made with farm-fresh cheese are Polish favorites. **Sernik** (sir-neek), or cheesecake, is a delicious example. It is made with a white cheese called **twarog** (tvahroog). Twarog is made with unpasteurized milk that is boiled with vinegar. Acid in the vinegar causes the milk to form curds and gives the cheese a slightly sour flavor.

Once the curds form, the cheese is squeezed to remove the liquid, or whey. The result can best be described as a cross between cream cheese and cottage cheese.

Twarog is easy to spread and good for baking. To turn it into cheesecake, Polish bakers mix it with butter, eggs, sugar, and flour. Often raisins, bits of candied orange peel, and/or sliced peaches are added to the cheese mixture, which sweetens the cake and gives it a fresh scent. The mixture is baked in a square or rectangular pan until the top browns. This type of cheesecake does not have a crust. Poles also make cheesecakes

Coffee

Poles enjoy sipping coffee while eating pastry. Coffee did not arrive in Poland until the late 17th century, when Polish King Jan Sobieski seized a bag of coffee beans from invading Turkish forces. At first, Poles considered coffee to be a foreign poison. As coffee drinking became popular in Germany and Austria, Poles became more interested in the drink. In 1724, a coffeehouse was opened in Warsaw. Soon, drinking coffee became popular with Polish nobility. As the price of coffee decreased, more Poles drank it, and coffeehouses were opened throughout Poland. By 1822, there were ninety coffee shops in Warsaw. They became a popular meeting place for Polish writers and artists. Many of these old coffeehouses are still in business today. They are elegant places with waiters who provide table service. Newer, more casual coffeehouses with counter service are also widespread.

Polish cheesecake, called sernik, is much denser than American cheesecake and usually has no crust. It is often topped with fresh berries, whipped cream, or chocolate (shown).

with thin crisp crusts. With or without a crust, sernik may be served plain or topped with fresh berries, whipped cream, or a layer of chocolate, which hardens as the cake cools.

Like all cheesecakes, sernik is quite rich. Because of twarog's slightly sour flavor, it is not as sweet as most western European or American cheesecakes. It is also denser. John Connolly, a blogger and Englishman living in Poland, explained: "I was never a fan of cheesecake in London...but it is a different story over here! Sernik was the first thing I ate in Poland when I arrived at my girlfriend's mother's house …after learning how to make this…I have made it any chance I can."[14]

Filled with Poppy Seeds

Other Polish pastries feature poppy seeds. Poppy seeds are small blue-gray seeds that come from **poppies**, bright red flowers that grow wild in Poland and are also often planted in home gardens. The seeds can be used whole, or they can be ground into a paste. They have a crunchy texture and a nut-like flavor.

Poles make sandwich cookies filled with poppy seed paste, and poppy seed–flavored coffee cakes. **Makowiec** (mak-oh-vee-ets) is far and away the most popular Polish pastry made with poppy seeds. It is a crusty,

Makowiec is a rolled cake made with poppy seeds and honey. It is a common dessert at holiday meals.

log-shaped pastry, filled with a sweet moist paste composed of poppy seeds, raisins, almonds, walnuts, candied orange peels, and honey. The honey, which comes from Polish wildflowers such as dandelions, buckwheat, or mustard flowers, is thicker, darker, and spicier than American honey. It gives the pastries a sweet warm flavor.

Poles have been using local honey as a sweetener for centuries. In the Middle Ages, they gathered wild honey from beehives in the forests. In later years, beekeeping became a common practice in Polish monasteries and farms. Today, it is an important industry in Poland. Polish honey is known for its purity, warm floral scent, and sweet-spicy flavor.

Combining the honey with fruits, nuts, and poppy seeds gives makowiec a mouth-watering aroma and a rich natural taste. Makowiec is usually topped with a glazed powdered sugar icing. It is often baked for Christmas and Easter dinners, but it is eaten throughout the year, too. "If you are Polish and grew up in a Polish or Eastern European household like myself," said Cathy, a Polish-American cook, "the word makowiec arouses a hunger for which there is no other substitution. A dessert table in my childhood would not have been complete without this roll."[15]

Just Add Fruit

Fruit-filled pastries are other popular desserts and snacks. Apples, plums, pears, sour cherries, and berries grow wild in Polish forests and are cultivated on Polish

Fruits, such as apples, are abundant in Poland, and are a favorite ingredient in desserts.

farms. Polish bakers take advantage of these local goodies in such delicacies as plum cake, strawberry shortcake, and fruit-filled tarts. Of all fruit-filled pastries, apple cake is probably the national favorite. Polish bakers make many different types of apple cakes. **Jablecznik** (yah-bwetch-neek) is a popular choice. It is a soft, spongy, two-layer cake. Tart apples that are sweetened with sugar and spiced with cloves are sandwiched between the layers. It has a fresh fragrance and a moist, light taste. "The apples make a scrumptious tart contrast to the sweetness of the cake," explained Polish cooking blogger Krissie. "I like to bake this cake in the summer months, because of the clean crisp flavours."[16]

Szarlotka (shahr-lawt-kah) is equally popular. It is more like an apple pie than a cake. It is similar to jablecznik in that it has an apple filling sandwiched between two layers of pastry. But the layers are made with thick

Apple Cake

This is a fragrant and tasty cake. The cake can be made in a large rectangular baking pan, a high round cake pan, or a Bundt pan. It may be topped with powdered sugar or whipped cream or served without a topping.

Ingredients
2 cups flour
2 eggs
½ cup applesauce
¾ cup sugar
1 teaspoon baking soda
1 tablespoon cinnamon
2 apples, peeled and shredded
⅓ cup chopped walnuts
1 cup raisins
1 cup vanilla yogurt

Instructions
1. Preheat the oven to 370°F.
2. Spray the baking pan with nonstick spray.
3. Mix together the applesauce, sugar, eggs, cinnamon, raisins, nuts, yogurt, and apples. Add the flour and baking soda and mix well. The batter should be a thick liquid.
4. Pour the batter into the pan. Bake until a fork put into the middle of the cake comes out dry, about 45 minutes.

Makes one cake. Serves 10.

dough that gives it a pie-like taste. Szarlotka is baked in a rectangular pan and topped with powdered sugar. I has a crunchy crust and a crisp, mildly sweet flavor. It is eaten warm or cold. Topping it with fresh whipped cream or vanilla ice cream makes it a special treat.

Fine Pastries

Kolachkies

Filled cookies known as kolachkies are traditional Polish treats. They are made with dough that contains cream cheese, which gives the cookie a light, flaky texture. The dough is rolled out until it is very thin. Then it is cut into a circle or square and filled with cheese, fruit jam, or poppy-seed paste, and folded into a pinwheel, diamond, or square shape.

There is some controversy about where these pastries originated. Poland, the Czech Republic, and Slovakia each takes credit. Throughout history Polish, Czech, and Slovakian people have had a lot of contact with each other. At one time, Poland conquered Bohemia, a section of the Czech Republic. And in the Middle Ages, Polish, Slovakian, and Czech royalty often married each other. Cooking styles and recipes were passed back and forth. No matter their birthplace, kolachkies are loved throughout central Europe.

Nut Treats

Like fruit, walnuts, hazelnuts, and chestnuts grow in abundance in Polish forests. They often are featured in Polish baked goods. Walnut and hazelnut cakes, nut coffee cakes, and cream-filled nut cakes are common additions to Polish tables. Almonds, too, are used frequently. **Mazurek** (mah-zoo-reek), a favorite Polish pastry, combines ground almonds, sugar, and egg whites to form a thin, crisp rectangular pastry base, almost like a large wafer. It is topped with a dizzying

Chocolate Mazurek

Poles like chocolate and nuts. This chocolate mazurek combines the two.

Ingredients
2 cups flour
1 cup dark chocolate chips, melted
½ cup butter
3 eggs
½ cup sugar
2 tablespoons milk
½ cup chopped walnuts

Instructions
1. Preheat oven to 350°F.
2. Spray a shallow square or rectangular baking pan with nonstick spray.
3. Mix together the butter, chocolate, and sugar. Add the eggs, milk, and flour. Mix well.
4. Pour the batter into the pan. Bake until a fork inserted in the middle of the cake comes away dry, about 20 minutes. Sprinkle the nuts on the top of the baked cake.

Makes one cake.
Serves 10.

Mazurek is a tasty dessert combining chocolate and nuts.

variety of fillings. The only limit is the baker's imagination. Fruit preserves; poppy-seed paste; dried fruit and walnuts; apple slices and hazelnuts; and chocolate and almonds are just a few of the many options. The filling may be sprinkled with chopped almonds or sweetened bread crumbs or it may be coated with chocolate or vanilla icing.

An elaborately decorated form of mazurek with the word "halleluiah" spelled out in icing is often served on Easter. Other varieties are eaten year-round. According to Pininska, "It is now an integral part of Polish cooking, with enough different kinds for each day of the year."[17] With its sweet, rich, crunchy taste, it is no wonder Poles cannot wait for a special occasion to eat it.

Mazurek, apple cakes, poppy-seed logs, and cheesecake are just a few of the many pastries that Poles enjoy as often as possible. There are also richly layered chocolate cakes, plump doughnuts oozing with jelly, light fluffy pancakes filled with jam, fruit-filled pound cakes, and sweet cupcakes frosted with sour cream. These and other yummy pastries make snacks and desserts extra special in Poland.

chapter 4

Food for the Holidays

Poles love to eat, socialize, and celebrate. Their hospitality is legendary. Holidays are a wonderful time to get together and share food with friends and family. Poles celebrate many holidays in much the same way as they did centuries ago. Traditional foods made for specific holidays are an important part of the celebration.

Christmas Specialties

The Christmas season is celebrated with much fanfare in Poland, with Christmas Eve being the most important day of the year. According to Polish tradition, whatever a person does on Christmas Eve, he or she will do for the upcoming year. So, people try to do good

There is always a ceremonial dinner, or wigilia, in Poland on Christmas Eve. Traditionally an extra place is set at the table for an unexpected guest, be it friend or stranger.

deeds and avoid trouble. The high point of the day is **wigilia** (vee-ghee-lah), a feast that is usually eaten before Poles attend midnight church services. Most Poles are Catholic. For religious reasons, many give up meat for Advent, a forty-day period that ends on Christmas Day. For this reason, wigilia is almost always a meatless meal.

There are many traditions connected with wigilia. For instance, an extra place setting is set out for unexpected guests or lonely travelers, because no one is supposed to eat wigilia alone. Friends, relatives, neighbors, and even strangers are welcome. In fact, an old Polish saying states, "A guest in the home is like God in the home."[18]

The meal usually has twelve courses, one for each month of the year. Before the food is served, a cracker known as **oplatek** (awp-wah-tek) is shared in a special ceremony in which everyone eats a piece and expresses

Sauerkraut and Apples

In Poland, salads and side dishes are a big part of holiday meals. This is a sweet and sour mixture that is served as a salad or vegetable dish. A shredded carrot and/or chopped onion can be added. It is best served cold.

Ingredients
2 cups sauerkraut
1 large apple, peeled and shredded
1 tablespoon sugar
3 tablespoons olive oil
½ teaspoon black pepper

Instructions
1. Put the sauerkraut in a colander. Rinse it with cool water. Put the sauerkraut between paper towels or a clean dish towel and squeeze out excess moisture.
2. Combine all the ingredients in a bowl. Mix well.
3. Cover the bowl and refrigerate for 1–2 hours.
Serves 4.

Pierniki

Pierniki (pyehr-nee-kee), or gingerbread cookies, have been a part of Polish Christmas celebrations since the 17th century. Gingerbread came to Poland from Germany. Because the spices used to make gingerbread were so expensive, at first it was only eaten by Polish royalty.

Early cookies were little works of art that depicted the daily lives of Polish noblemen and women. With the help of intricately designed wooden molds, gingerbread dough was shaped into women in long gowns, men dressed for hunting, horse-drawn carriages, and castles.

In the 18th century, simpler molds came into use. Gingerbread cookies related to Christmas became popular. Modern Polish gingerbread cookies depict angels, Santa Claus, Christmas trees, animals, and hearts. They are decorated with icing and are given out as treats to Christmas carolers. Poles often exchange heart-shaped gingerbread cookies.

Little gingerbread cookies called pierniki are cut in many different shapes.

their best wishes for each other. Then, the feasting begins. Menus vary, but certain dishes are likely to be served.

Barszcz (bah-rsh-ch), a deep red beet soup, is a popular first course. The soup is made from pickled or fermented beets and has a crisp sour taste. Poles have been eating barszcz on Christmas Eve since the 16th century.

A variety of fish dishes comes next. Carp, a freshwater fish that is very popular in Poland, is a traditional

Baked Fish with Cheese

Whitefish topped with melted cheese is a simple dish that is popular in Poland. Flounder, tilapia, or sole are good fish to use.

Ingredients
4 flounder fillets
¼ teaspoon each of salt and pepper
2 tablespoons bread crumbs
½ cup grated cheddar cheese
½ cup butter, melted
1 teaspoon chopped parsley

Instructions
1. Preheat the oven to 350°F.
2. Spray a baking pan with nonstick spray.
3. Put the fish in the pan. Sprinkle with salt and pepper. Pour the butter on top of the fish. Top with bread crumbs and cheese.
4. Cook until the cheese is melted and the fish is flaky, about 15 minutes.
Serves 4.

choice. Because carp live on the bottom of ponds and lakes and feed on sewage, they are considered "dirty" fish in many parts of the world—but not in Poland. Here, grain-fed carp have been raised in specially cleaned ponds since the 12th century. Usually, the Polish cook buys a live carp for wigilia. The fish is kept in a large tub until it is killed and cooked. As the fish swims around the tub, any sand or mud on its body is cleaned off. Poles say that eating carp is good luck. In the past, it was almost always served whole with the head on. Modern cooks are more likely to cut up the fish and fry, bake, or boil it and top it with chopped hard-boiled eggs and lemon juice.

Other courses often include noodles with poppy seeds, cabbage stuffed with mushrooms, a variety of pierogi filled with sauerkraut, cheese, potatoes, and/or mushrooms, and **kutia** (koo-tee-ah), an old-fashioned Polish Christmas pudding. Poles say that eating it brings people wealth. Although this outcome is unlikely, eating the pudding on wigilia is customary. Kutia is made with poppy seeds, honey, fruit jam, walnuts, raisins, and boiled wheat berries, which are whole kernels of wheat. Kutia is served cold, topped with heavy cream. It is sweet and hearty, more like porridge in taste and texture than smooth, creamy pudding.

Butter, Cream, Eggs, and Sugar

Tradition is also alive in Poland before Easter. Many Poles observe Lent, a forty-day period prior to Easter in which people give up meat, eggs, sugar, and dairy products for religious reasons. To clear their homes of these foods, on Fat Tuesday, the day before Lent begins, Poles eat foods rich in eggs, sugar, and dairy products. **Paczki** (paunch-kee), plump, sugary dough-nuts oozing with jam are always a part of this pre-Lenten ritual. "I love this Polish custom, as it involves something sweet and delicious!" Krissie explained.

Paczki are a plump pastries filled with jam that are traditionally enjoyed on Fat Tuesday, the day before Lent begins.

"In Poland... Fat Tuesday and authentic paczki recipes go hand in hand."[19]

Paczki are round doughnuts without holes. They originated in the 17th century. At that time, they were filled with plum jam. Today they may be filled with almond paste or apricot, cherry, plum, or prune jams. They contain lots of eggs and butter and are very light and fluffy. Reverend Jedrzej Kitowicz , an 18th-century Polish writer, described them as: "So plump and light that if you squeeze one in your hand it springs back to its original size like a sponge and a light wind would whisk it off the platter."[20]

Easter Foods

After forty days without favorite foods, Poles look forward to Easter dinner with great anticipation. Many Polish cooks begin preparing on Good Friday, two days before Easter. Their goal is to cook enough food to fill a basket by Saturday afternoon. Poles take the baskets to church for the priest to bless. Although contents vary, hard-boiled eggs, sausage, and bread are usually included. The meat symbolizes wealth; the eggs, new life; and the bread, home and family.

On Easter, the blessed food, plus lots of other foods, are placed on the dining table, which is often decorated with beautifully colored Easter eggs. The centerpiece is the Easter lamb. It is not an actual cooked lamb, but rather, a lamb sculpted out of butter or cake. A special mold is used to make the lamb.

Lambs have been connected with Easter for centuries. Poles first started making butter lambs in the 14th century. In later years, cake lambs became popular. The lamb is quite a work of art. It is usually placed atop a bed of greens to resemble a lamb in a pasture. Candies form its eye, nose, and mouth, and a little paper banner with the sign of the cross is stuck in the lamb's back.

The meal itself is likely to include ham, sausage, stuffed cabbage, pierogi, freshly baked bread, salads, and potatoes. **Babka** (bahb-kah), a special cake, is almost always the dessert. The word babka means *old woman* or *grandmother* in Polish. Many people say the cake got its name because its shape resembles the long, wide, pleated skirts that Polish grandmothers use to wear.

A babka's shape is very important. It is usually made in a tall fluted pan. The taller and plumper the cake is, the better. Writer Judy McCann, whose family is Polish, explained: "My grandmother always told me that a housewife's reputation as a cook rests on the successful rising of her babka."[21] Since heat helps dough to rise, in the past, the dough was covered with a fluffy down comforter to keep it warm. Windows and doors were kept closed while the dough was rising. In an effort to prevent any loud noises that might cause the dough to fall while the cake was baking, family members tiptoed around the kitchen.

A perfect babka is a Polish baker's delight. The golden yellow cake is made with yeast and plenty of

The day before Easter Poles gather symbolic foods in a basket to be blessed by a priest. On Easter the blessed food is served as a part of the meal.

Polish Easter Eggs

Pisanki, brightly colored, intricately decorated Easter eggs, are a part of Polish Easter celebrations. Egg decorating is an art form in Poland that is passed down from mothers to daughters. Polish Easter eggs are colored with natural dyes from plant products such as beet or onion skins. They are decorated with symbols of Easter such as crosses and lambs; with Easter greetings; or with floral or geometric designs. Every region of Poland has its own designs. The designs are scratched into the surface of the egg or they are piped on with hot wax. Eggs are also decorated with cut paper and bits of straw, which are glued onto the eggs. The eggs are often exchanged between friends and relatives.

Polish hand-painted wooden eggs are also well known. These eggs may be the same size as actual eggs or larger. They are collected by people throughout the world.

Brightly colored and elaborately decorated Easter eggs are a part of Polish Easter.

butter, sugar, and egg yolks. In fact, some babka recipes call for two dozen egg yolks. The cake also usually contains raisins and candied orange peel and may have sugary crumbs, fruit syrup, or chocolate icing on top. The end result is a dense, flaky, gorgeous cake that is a Polish tradition.

Traditional foods like babka are a big part of Polish culture. Celebrating important holidays in time-honored ways gives the Polish people a chance to share special foods with each other while staying connected to their past. In this way, they keep their history alive.

Metric Conversions

Mass (weight)

1 ounce (oz.)	= 28.0 grams (g)
8 ounces	= 227.0 grams
1 pound (lb.) or 16 ounces	= 0.45 kilograms (kg)
2.2 pounds	= 1.0 kilogram

Liquid Volume

1 teaspoon (tsp.)	= 5.0 milliliters (ml)
1 tablespoon (tbsp.)	= 15.0 milliliters
1 fluid ounce (oz.)	= 30.0 milliliters
1 cup (c.)	= 240 milliliters
1 pint (pt.)	= 480 milliliters
1 quart (qt.)	= 0.96 liters (l)
1 gallon (gal.)	= 3.84 liters

Pan Sizes

8- inch cake pan	= 20 x 4-centimeter cake pan
9-inch cake pan	= 23 x 3.5-centimeter cake pan
11 x 7-inch baking pan	= 28 x 18-centimeter baking pan
13 x 9-inch baking pan	= 32.5 x 23-centimeter baking pan
9 x 5-inch loaf pan	= 23 x 13-centimeter loaf pan
2-quart casserole	= 2-liter casserole

Temperature

212° F	= 100° C (boiling point of water)
225° F	= 110° C
250° F	= 120° C
275° F	= 135° C
300° F	= 150° C
325° F	= 160° C
350° F	= 180° C
375° F	= 190° C
400° F	= 200° C

Length

1/4 inch (in.)	= 0.6 centimeters (cm)
1/2 inch	= 1.25 centimeters
1 inch	= 2.5 centimeters

Notes

Chapter 1: What the Land Has to Offer

1. Sophie Hodorowicz Knab, *The Polish Country Kitchen Cookbook*. New York: Hippocrene Books, 2002. p. 252.

2. Michal, "Polish Bread," The Polski Blog, November 16, 2008, http://thepolskiblog.co.uk/2008/11/polish-bread/.

3. Mat, "It's Time for Mushrooms—A Real Autumn Dinner," *Tasting Poland*, September 13, 2010, www.tastingpoland.com/blog/autumn_dinner.html.

4. Mary Pininska, *The Polish Kitchen*. London: Grub Street, 2000. p. 93.

5. Michal, "Smalec—Poland's Favourite Starter," *The Polski Blog*, October 11, 2008, http://thepolskiblog.co.uk/2008/10/smalec-polands-favourite-starter/.

Chapter 2: Delicious and Hearty

6. Kamila_2, "Traditional and Lesser Known Foods of Poland," *Polish forums*, www.polishforums.com/food-drink-8/traditional-lesser known-foods-poland-11394/.

7. Rysia, *Old Warsaw Cookbook*. New York: Hippocrene Books, 1999. p. 9.

8. Barbara Sweich, "Krupnik Soup Recipe," *Bella Online*, www.bellaonline.com/articles/art170429.asp.

9. Quoted in Sophie Hodorowicz Knab, *The Polish Country Kitchen Cookbook*. p. 99.

10. Krissie, "Pierogi Recipe," *Polish Girls Can Cook*, December 1, 2010, http://polishcooking.blogspot.com/search?updated-max=2010-12-14T21%3A29%3A00-08%3A00&max-results=7.

11. Knab, *The Polish Country Kitchen Cookbook*. p. 267.

12. Richard A. Slowik, "Stuffed Cabbage Golabki—No Doubt About it, I Like A Lot of Stuffing," *Spuscizna*, http://spuscizna.org/spuscizna/golabki.html.

Chapter 3: Fine Pastries

13. Alina Zeranska, *The Art of Polish Cooking.* Gretna, Louisiana: Pelican Publishing Co, 1996. p. 275.

14. John Connolly, "Sernik (Polish Cheesecake) Recipe," *Polish Food and Recipes,* July 27, 2007, http://polishfoodrecipes.blogspot.com/2007/07/sernik-polish-cheesecake-recipe.html.

15. Cathy, "Poppyseed Roll (Makowiec)," *Noble Pig,* September 5, 2010, http://noblepig.com/2010/09/04/poppyseed-roll-makowiec.aspx.

16. Krissie, "Jablecznik—Polish Apple Cake Recipe" *Polish Girls Can Cook,* September 19, 2010, http://polishcooking.blogspot.com/2010/09/jablecznik-polish-apple-cake-recipe.html.

17. Pininska, *The Polish Kitchen.* p. 172.

Chapter 4: Food for the Holidays

18. Knab, *The Polish Country Kitchen Cookbook.* p. 126.

19. Krissie, "Lent—Fat Thursday and Delicious Paczki/Doughnuts," *Polish Girls Can Cook,* February 24, 2011, http://polishcooking.blogspot.com/.

20. Quoted in Knab, *The Polish Country Kitchen Cookbook.* p.141.

21. Judy McCann, "Memories of a Polish Easter," *Global Gourmet,* www.globalgourmet.com/destinations/poland/poleaster.html#axzz1Ix5pjcvH.

Glossary

amber: Hard yellow fossilized tree sap used to make jewelry.

babka: A tall round fluted cake.

barszcz: Beet soup.

bigos (hunter's stew): A hearty stew often made with wild game.

ferments: A chemical process in which sugar is converted to alcohol.

golabki: Cabbage leaves stuffed with rice and meat.

jablecznik: A soft, spongy two-layer cake.

kapusniak: Cabbage soup.

kielbasa: A Polish sausage.

krupnik: Barley soup.

kutia: Polish Christmas pudding.

makowiec: A sweet log-shaped pastry filled with poppy-seed paste.

marjoram: A fragrant herb with small leaves and a sweet spicy taste.

mazurek: Polish pastry made with ground almonds and a variety of fillings.

oplatek: A cracker served before wigilia.

paczki: Doughnuts without holes that are filled with fruit preserves.

pierogi: Stuffed half-moon–shaped dumplings.

poppies: Bright red flowers; a source of poppy seeds used in cooking.

sernik: Polish cheesecake.

smalec: Pig fat.

szarlotka: Dessert that has apple filling between two layers of pastry.

torte: Layer cake.

twarog: Polish white cheese.

uszka: Tiny dumplings filled with meat or mushrooms

wigilia: Christmas Eve dinner.

zupa: Soup.

For Further Exploration

Books

Zilah Decker, *National Geographic Countries of the World: Poland.* Des Moines, Iowa: 2008. Looks at Polish history, geography, politics, and famous citizens with beautiful photographs and maps.

Charlotte Guillain, *Poland.* Chicago: Heinemann Educational Books, 2011. Looks at Polish history, geography, and daily life.

Sean McCollum, *Poland.* Minneapolis: Lerner Books, 2008. Information on Poland's people, language, daily life, religion, and geography.

Kathleen Pohl, *Poland.* London: Franklin Watts, Ltd. 2010. A simple book that takes readers on a tour of Poland with lots of information and photos.

Websites

Central Intelligence Agency, "The World Factbook, Poland," (https://www.cia.gov/library/publications/the-world-factbook/geos/pl.html). Information about Polish geography, government, current issues, economy, and people that includes a map and photos.

Kids Konnect, "Poland," (http://www.kidskonnect .com/subject-index/26-countriesplaces/329-poland .html). Presents fast facts about Poland and many links for additional information.

National Geographic Kids, "Poland," (http://kids .nationalgeographic.com/kids/places/find/poland/). Lots of information about Poland including a video, map, and e-postcards.

Index

Picture Credits

About the Author

Barbara Sheen is the author of more than sixty books for young people. She lives in New Mexico with her family. In her spare time, she likes to swim, garden, read, and walk. Of course, she loves to cook!